The Tramways of the South Midlands
(Networks Edition)

The aim of this series of booklets is to set down in concise form the history and geography of Britain's tramways, taking as the starting-point the regional chapters of *Great British Tramway Networks*. This book by W. H. Bett and J. C. Gillham has been out of print for many years, but is still in demand, and much more information has come to light since it was published.

One of its chapters was titled "The Isolated Outposts" and dealt with those systems (from Guernsey to Carlisle) which had no near tramway neighbour. A dozen of these were in the area between London, the North Midlands, and the Severn, and form a convenient geographical group for a regional book, to which we have given the title of *The Tramways of the South Midlands*. More precisely, it covers the counties of Northamptonshire, Bedfordshire, Buckinghamshire, Oxfordshire, Berkshire, Wiltshire, Gloucestershire, Worcestershire, and the southern part of Warwickshire.

The arrangement of the tramway systems is in a mainly-geographical clockwise progression, starting with Northampton and proceeding through Wolverton, Luton, Oxford, Reading, Wantage, Swindon, Gloucester, Cheltenham and Worcester to finish at Leamington Spa. Mention will also be made of proposed tramways that were not built, and certain narrow-gauge railways.

Northampton

Northampton's local transport was typical of many, in being provided firstly by company-owned horse trams, and then (from soon after the turn of the century) by municipal electric trams which ran until the 1930s. The Northampton Street Tramways Company introduced 3ft 6in gauge horse trams to Kingsley Park in 1881, Kingsthorpe in 1883, St. James in 1884, and Abington Park in 1893, working from a depot in Abington Street on the site of the present library. There were 18 double-deck and four single-deck horse cars on 5¼ miles of route.

Northampton Corporation bought out the company in 1901, and electrified the four routes on the same gauge in 1904, with short extensions at two of the termini and a new depot at St. James. A fifth route, to Far Cotton, was opened in 1914 (replacing a horse bus service) after agreement had been reached with the LNWR for a tramway/railway level crossing at Northampton (Bridge Street) station. 10 miles of route were authorised, of which 6.42 were built. A cross-suburban trolleybus route linking three tram termini was authorised in 1911, but not constructed. There were 33 four-wheel cars of open-top and enclosed types, also four quite modern bogie single-deckers delivered in December 1921. Municipal motor buses replaced the trams in 1929-34.

COVER PICTURE: Northampton 34 at the builder's works in 1921.　　　(T&RW

Horse tram No. 4 of the Northampton Street Tramways Company in Abington Street. The horse trams were replaced by Corporation electric trams in 1904. *(TMS*

Wellingborough and Bedford

The County of Northampton Electric Power and Traction Company, Ltd., a subsidiary of the British Electric Traction Company, obtained in 1900 the Wellingborough and District Tramroads Act for a standard-gauge tramway from Wellingborough to Rushden by two routes (via Finedon and via Irchester), with a branch from Higham Ferrers to Raunds, plus local routes in Wellingborough and Rushden. The total would have been nearly 19 miles, but the powers were allowed to lapse.

The same fate also befell the Act obtained in 1900 by Bedford Corporation for 8.9 route miles of 3ft 6in gauge electric tramway on ten short routes radiating from Bedford town centre, with a depot in Cauldwell Road. An 1892 Act of the Bedford and Kempston Tramway Co. Ltd. for a 3ft 6in line from Bedford Midland Station to Kempston High Street had also fallen through.

Newport Pagnell

The Newport Pagnell and District Tramways Company was empowered in 1887 to link that place with Olney by a steam tramway, again on the 3ft 6in gauge, 6.14 miles long. Five-sixths of the track was laid, and a new bridge built over the river Ouse, but work then ceased because the Board of Trade refused to permit the tramway to run along the main street of Emberton village and the company was unable to purchase any land for a reserved-track bypass. Buckinghamshire County Council obtained an Act authorising them to remove the rails in 1893.

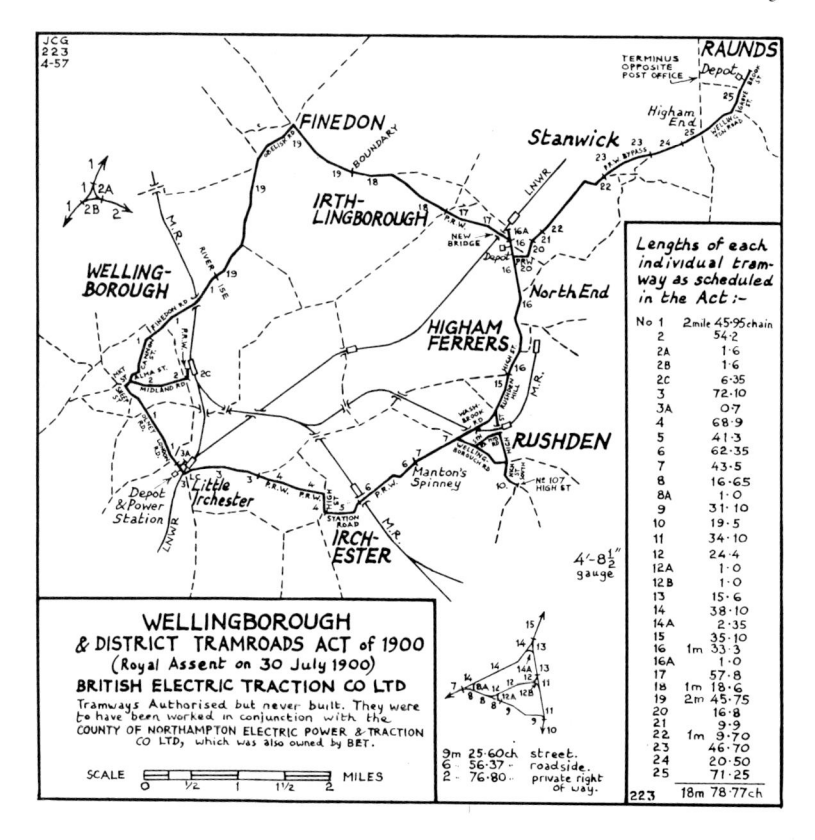

Wolverton

A 2.67-mile steam tramway promoted and owned by a sequence of companies which had six different titles from 1882 to 1919 linked Wolverton with Stony Stratford on the 3ft 6in gauge from 1887 onwards. There was also a short-lived 2-mile extension to Deanshanger in 1888/89, built in anticipation of goods traffic which never materialised. Most of the passengers were workmen employed at the LNWR (later LMSR) Wolverton carriage works or at McCorquodale's printing works. They rode in huge double-deck trailer cars (three 100-seaters, one 80-seater, and one 50-seater) which, unusually for British steam tramways, were permitted to run in coupled pairs; there were also two smaller cars, and three steam engines. The line was purchased by two Trustees on behalf of the LNWR on 26 February 1920, and closed down by the LMSR in 1926 because of the General Strike. It was bought and lifted by Bucks. County Council in 1927.

Luton

The town of Luton had electric trams on five short standard-gauge local routes until 1932. They did not start until 1908, being leased at first to J. G. White & Co.

Luton Corporation No. 3 on a test run in New Bedford Road, early in 1908.
(Courtesy A. D. Packer

Ltd., from whom the lease was taken over in 1909 by Balfour Beatty & Co. Ltd. The routes totalled 5¼ miles, and a further 1.45 miles authorised in 1905 was not built; this would have taken the trams along Leagrave Road to Biscot, and to Luton Hoo park gates. The tracks were always owned by Luton Corporation, who took over direct operation in 1923. The Eastern National Omnibus Company agreed to take over and replace the tram service in 1930, but the Minister of Transport refused to allow this, and the trams were instead replaced in 1932 by municipal motor buses. The thirteen trams (twelve four-wheel double-deckers and one single-decker) were sold for £50 the lot, and the bus undertaking was sold in January 1970 to the United Counties Omnibus Co. Ltd.

An unsuccessful application had been made in 1902 and again in 1903 by a group who planned to form the Luton, Dunstable and District Light Railway Company, with powers for five Luton routes, one of which would have continued through Dunstable to Houghton Regis. Both applications were for 10 miles of standard gauge route, but both were rejected due to objections by the Great Northern Railway. Many years later, in 1989, the local Luton & District bus company (successor to United Counties) drew up a scheme to run modern trams, or alternatively guided buses, on the recently-closed ex-GNR railway from Dunstable to Luton, possibly continuing to Luton airport.

Hemel Hempstead

In 1880 a scheme was promoted for a "Chesham, Boxmoor, and Hemel Hempstead Tramways" with 8.34 miles of 4ft 8½in gauge line, but no more was heard of this. Similar schemes, with steam traction, were promoted in 1888 on the 3ft 6in gauge and in 1889 on standard gauge. These were rejected, but were revived eleven years later in the form of a more modest "Hemel Hempstead Tramways" with three routes totalling 3.09 miles linking Hemel Hempstead with Boxmoor Station and Apsley Mills. In 1900 Hertfordshire County Council applied for three almost identical routes, but both schemes were rejected. Parliament had also been asked in 1888 to sanction the "Tring and Aylesbury Tramways" with 8.7 miles of 3ft 6in gauge steam line along the grass verge of the main road between those two towns, and eastwards to Tring Station, but this also fell through.

Wotton (Brill)

In the west of Buckinghamshire, the Duke of Buckingham built and owned the Wotton Tramway, opened in 1871 from Quainton Road station on the Aylesbury and Buckingham Railway to serve his estate at Wotton and the village of Brill, being a standard-gauge line 6½ miles long with a 1½ mile branch to Moat Farm. A passenger service was provided on the main line from 1872, when the horses were replaced by an unusual geared steam locomotive built by Aveling & Porter of Rochester. The line changed hands in 1883, becoming the Oxford and Aylesbury Tramroad Company, and in 1888 the O&AT obtained an Act authorising an eleven-mile extension south-westwards to Oxford (Magdalen Bridge). Another Act in 1894 slightly altered half of the route, but none of it was built. From 1899 the main line was worked by the Metropolitan Railway as a part of their system, and was closed in 1935. The Moat Farm branch closed in 1910.

Oxford

At Magdalen Bridge, Oxford, the O&AT would have met the original route of the City of Oxford and District Tramways Co. Ltd., which was opened from Cowley Road to the Railway Stations in 1881 on the 4ft gauge. Further horse routes were opened along Banbury Road in 1882, Walton Street in 1884, Abingdon Road to Hinksey in 1887 and further along Banbury Road to Summertown in 1898. The first eight cars were single-deck, but all later additions and replacements were double-deck, the maximum fleet being 20 cars.

Horse trams ran in Oxford from 1881 to 1914, but plans to introduce electric trams were unsuccessful. This horse car is seen in St. Giles Street near the Martyrs' Memorial.
(TMS

Oxford was never destined to have electric trams, though not through want of trying. The National Electric Construction Co. Ltd. obtained control of the tramways and set up the City of Oxford Electric Tramways Limited in 1906, which took over the horse trams in 1908. The intended electrification would have been on the Dolter surface-contact system, with tracks widened to standard gauge and route mileage increased from 5¼ to 14.42. By 1908 the Dolter system as adopted elsewhere was considered a failure, and plans were changed to be conduit supply in the centre and overhead further out, or to the cheaper option of petrol-electric trams which would take current from overhead wires on the outer sections of line but be self-propelled in the city centre. Negotiations between company and corporation continued for another six years, but the end came in 1914 after a rival concern headed by William Morris of Morris Motors started running Daimler motor buses, and the tramway company quickly followed suit, changing its name in 1921 to City of Oxford Motor Services, Limited, which still exists today.

Reading

Compared with Oxford, Reading's tramways were both uneventful and successful. The Reading Tramways Company Ltd. worked 4ft gauge horse cars, of which there were eventually thirteen, on the inner part of the town's main east-west route (2.37 miles) from 1879 until municipalisation in 1901 and electrification in 1903. Reading Corporation replaced and extended them with seven 4ft gauge routes (7.45 miles) traversing the main London, Bath, Oxford and Wokingham Roads and also serving Caversham Bridge, Whitley and Erleigh Road. All the cars were open-toppers, six being on bogies and thirty on four wheels. They were scrapped gradually during 1930-39, the last five routes being replaced by trolleybuses, and this system was later greatly extended to the south and west, but motor buses took over in 1965-68. Trolleybus powers for five feeder routes had originally been obtained in 1914, but were not exercised.

The Wantage Tramway, linking the town of Wantage with the Great Western Railway Wantage Road station, was Britain's first steam tramway. It carried passengers from 1875 to 1925, and goods until 1946. This c.1905 scene is at Grove Bridge.
(Chapman, Dawlish

Swindon No. 7 descending the 1 in 14 gradient in Victoria Road. (TMS

Wantage

From Wantage Town to Wantage Road Station (GWR) a 2½ mile standard-gauge horse tramway was opened by the Wantage Tramway Co. Ltd. in 1875. This rural roadside line was a suitable place to demonstrate mechanical traction, and in 1876 became the very first regular steam passenger tramway in the United Kingdom. The pioneer Grantham double-deck knifeboard-seat steam tramcar of 1872 with the boiler mounted amidships was operated from 1876 to 1890, and seven different steam locomotives were used over the years; one, now 134 years old, has been preserved. Two Mekarski compressed-air locomotives also ran for three months in 1880. There were seven passenger cars of different types, two of which had originally been built for display at exhibitions. The passenger service was replaced by motor buses on 31 July 1925, being almost the last as well as the first British steam tramway, but goods operation continued for another 20½ years.

Swindon

Swindon Corporation worked three short local electric routes on the 3ft 6in gauge from 1904 until 1929, radiating from near the GWR station to Rodbourne, Gorse Hill, and Old Town (Corn Exchange). Only 3.70 miles was actually built, although 8.2 miles had been authorised in 1901 plus a further 0.7 miles in 1904. There were thirteen four-wheel open-top cars of conventional design, one of which ran away and overturned on 1 June 1906, in the only serious accident to occur on any tramway in this book; five passengers died and at least 34 were injured. The tramways were managed jointly with the electricity undertaking, whose profits made good the loss on the trams.

Ten miles northwest of Swindon is the Cotswold Water Park at South Cerney, where a metre-gauge light railway was built in 1973 and worked by a diesel locomotive hauling up to three four-wheel trailer trams. These were purchased from Charleroi in Belgium, but the line ran for only two seasons and the trams were then sold to the Shane's Castle Railway near Antrim, in Northern Ireland, where they run today on the 3ft gauge.

Stroud

In 1902 Thomas Nevins, who owned the Cheltenham tramway system, applied for a Light Railway Order for 28¼ miles of 3ft 6in gauge electric lines radiating from the town of Stroud to Chalford, Nailsworth and Stonehouse, with a long interurban route via Pitchcombe, Painswick, the Cross Hands Inn and Shurdington to join the Cheltenham tramways, and a branch from the Cross Hands via Brockworth and Hucclecote to Gloucester. This was rejected, and Nevins then sought the authority of Parliament. Powers to create a Stroud and District Tramways Company and build 15.4 miles were granted by Act of 1903, but Painswick to Cheltenham was rejected. Gloucester County Council obtained a Light Railway Order in 1903 for the section from the Cross Hands to the city boundary, but none of the authorised lines were built. The Stroud company also applied in 1903 for trolleybus powers, which if granted and exercised would possibly have been the first such installation in Britain.

Gloucester

The City of Gloucester Tramways Company, Ltd., worked 14 horse cars from 1879 to 1902 on six short 4ft gauge routes totalling 3.40 miles. Gloucester Corporation replaced and extended them in 1904 with municipal electric tramways of 3ft 6in gauge totalling 7.05 miles along the six main roads leading out of the town. An additional 2.07 miles beyond Wotton of the route to Brockworth via Hucclecote were leased from the Gloucestershire County Council, the only British example of a county owning a tramway other than in the Lanarkshire, London, and Swansea areas. The short route to Westgate Bridge was abandoned in 1917 and its rails were used to build a siding into the GWR station yard and to extend the Hucclecote tramway to the Brockworth aircraft factory, special trams being used to convey building materials and aircraft parts. A further ¾ mile of tramway was laid inside the factory grounds. Gloucester's 30 trams were abandoned in 1927-33 in favour of municipal motor buses, whose operations were taken over on a 21-year lease in 1936 by the Bristol company.

Gloucester was also the home of a tramcar manufacturer and railway wagon builder, the Gloucester Railway Carriage and Wagon Company, Ltd., who made horse trams for Gloucester and electric trams for Cheltenham and Glasgow. The firm's most unusual order was for the 1896 "Daddy-Long-Legs" car of the Brighton and Rottingdean Seashore Electric Tramroad. From 1913 to 1956 the works built several hundred cars for the London Underground railways and for Toronto, but the company's principal activity was always the building and hiring of wagons, especially for the South Wales collieries. Rolling stock construction ceased in 1968, but the company still makes goods wagon bogies.

Stroud Road junction on the Gloucester Corporation Light Railways, with car No. 2 from Tuffley and car No. 14 going to Bristol Road. *(Lens of Sutton)*

Cheltenham

Cheltenham was not served by horse trams, but became the first town in the area of this book to have an electric tramway. Thomas Nevins obtained powers for 12.60 miles in 1900-04, and from 1901-05 the Cheltenham and District Light Railway Company ran 20 cars on 10.44 miles 3ft 6in gauge routes from Lansdown to Charlton Kings, to Leckhampton, and to Cleeve Hill. The latter was by far the longest route, including much roadside sleeper track. Cleeve Hill includes a 1 in 10 gradient, and suffered a runaway even before the start of public service, so on the outer part of this route passengers were not allowed to ride on the top deck, being obliged to ride 'inside' or change to an accompanying single-decker.

The Cheltenham company was owned locally until 1914 by T. Nevins & Sons, and then became part of the Balfour Beatty group, who in 1929 announced the intention to replace the trams with trolleybuses. This was narrowly rejected, and the three tram routes were replaced by motor buses in 1930. The company was taken over by the Red & White group in 1939, and in 1950 it became a subsidiary of the Bristol Tramways company.

Malvern and Hereford

A Light Railway Order was granted in 1911 for a $\tfrac{3}{8}$-mile 3ft 6in gauge funicular railway from Malvern to the 1395 ft summit of the Worcestershire Beacon. This was not built, but the idea was revived in 1961-62 in the form of a cableway or chairlift. This did not materialise, and the only chairlift which can feature in this book is the 1972 one in the grounds of Woburn Abbey in Bedfordshire. Eighteen miles west of Malvern, and back in 1880, the City of Hereford Tramways Company promoted a Bill for 3.87 miles of 3ft 6in gauge horse or steam tramways a short way along the Ross, Newent, Bromyard, Leominster and Kington roads, but this was not passed, and no electric tramway proposals for Hereford are known.

Worcester tram No. 10 entering the single track in Broad Street on the Malvern Road route, about 1907. *(Commercial Postcard)*

Worcester

Horse tramways were introduced at Worcester in 1884, with six cars on 3.27 miles of 3ft gauge routes to Barbourne, Bransford Road, and Shrub Hill Station. They cannot have been very profitable, for they had five successive owners, and the Shrub Hill service was often suspended. Plans for a fourth route to Bath Road did not proceed, due to the cost of widening the High Street. The post-1894 owners (The Worcester Tramways Limited) added horse bus services and excursions, and in 1897 offered to electrify the tramways, but the Corporation in 1899 accepted an alternative offer from the BET, who in 1902 set up The Worcester Electric Traction Co. Ltd.

Electric trams on the 3ft 6in gauge began running in early 1904, with routes to Barbourne, Astwood Cemetery via Rainbow Hill, Shrub Hill Station, London Road, Bath Road, and St. Johns. The St. Johns route was extended in 1906 along Malvern Road to the Brunswick Arms, bringing the total to 5.86 miles. Light Railway Orders were obtained in 1901-02 for 6.09 miles of country routes to Powick and Kempsey, but these were not built, and nor were short proposed extensions to Red Hill, Henwick Road and School Lane. There were 17 open-top four-wheeled cars, all having slipper brakes because of gradients in Rainbow Hill and London Road. Motor buses took over the country horse-bus routes in 1912. The Corporation, which had powers to buy the tramways in 1929, proposed to replace them with municipal trolleybuses, but changed their minds in 1928 and accepted an offer by the Birmingham and Midland Motor Omnibus Co. Ltd. (Midland Red) to provide town bus services on a 21-year lease, which was subsequently renewed. The Corporation did buy the tramways, but only to dismantle them.

Stratford and Moreton

Some 22 miles east of Worcester lies Stratford-on-Avon, which never had electric trams, either actual or proposed. However, there was for many years an ancient roadside 4 ft gauge horse tramway of 1826 from Stratford-on-Avon to Moreton-in-the-Marsh, 17 miles, with a 2½ mile branch of 1836 from Darlingscott to Shipston-on-Stour. It was more than just an industrial tramroad, for it also had a regular passenger service, otherwise it would not appear in this book. Moreton to Shipston became a normal GWR steam railway in 1889, but horses continued to work the 10½ mile section into Stratford to about 1904, and the track was not lifted until 1918.

Leamington and Warwick

Eight miles north-east from Stratford is Warwick, where the Leamington and Warwick Tramways and Omnibus Co., Ltd., worked a three-mile standard-gauge horse-tram service between these twin towns from 1882 to 1905, with eight double-deck cars. In 1899 its share capital was purchased by the BET, who changed the company's name in 1902 to Leamington and Warwick Electrical Company, Limited, and introduced electric cars on the 3ft 6in gauge. The company also generated and sold electricity for domestic and industrial use from its power station near the tram depot, coal being hauled from the GWR sidings by a four-wheel steeple-cab electric locomotive. The thirteen open-top trams were replaced in 1930 by the same company's motor buses, after a trolleybus Bill had been rejected in 1928. Meanwhile, the company was sold in 1912 to the Balfour Beatty group, but the transport part was re-purchased in 1935 by the BET group's Midland Red subsidiary, the title having meanwhile been changed to Leamington & Warwick Transport Company, Ltd.

Other Minor Lines

Narrow-gauge passenger railways exist in several places in the area of this book. The oldest is probably the line at Wicksteed Park, Kettering, which opened in 1931, though the 2ft gauge Leighton Buzzard Narrow Gauge Railway began as an industrial line in 1919 but did not carry passengers until the 1960s. A busy 2ft 6in gauge line, opened in 1970, takes visitors to see the animals at Whipsnade Zoo near Dunstable, and there is a 15-inch gauge line in the grounds of Blenheim Palace. A metre-gauge railway representing the former ironstone tramways is being built in the Country Park at Irchester in Northamptonshire. Many British narrow gauge railways have used 'Simplex' petrol or diesel locomotives made by the Motor Rail and Tramcar Company, Ltd., of Bedford, but the Tramcars of this title were mostly for Karachi.

In recent years the bodies of several of the trams we have mentioned have been rescued from fields and farmyards in the hope that they can eventually be restored and preserved. They include four electric cars (Cheltenham 21, Luton 6, Northampton 21 and Swindon 13) and five horse cars, two each from Leamington and Oxford and one from Gloucester. The Leamington cars are kept at the Birmingham Railway Museum at Tyseley, and those from Oxford are at the Oxford Bus Museum at Long Hanborough. Parts of two Wolverton and Stony Stratford steam tram trailers are at the Milton Keynes rural life museum at Wolverton.

There is also a possibility that trams may return to Gloucester in a new form. The city is considering a plan for a one-way city-centre distributor loop, to provide a transport service along pedestrianised shopping streets and link them with car parks and the museum complex in Gloucester Docks. The gauge would be 4ft 8½in and cars would be hired from museums pending the construction of replicas.

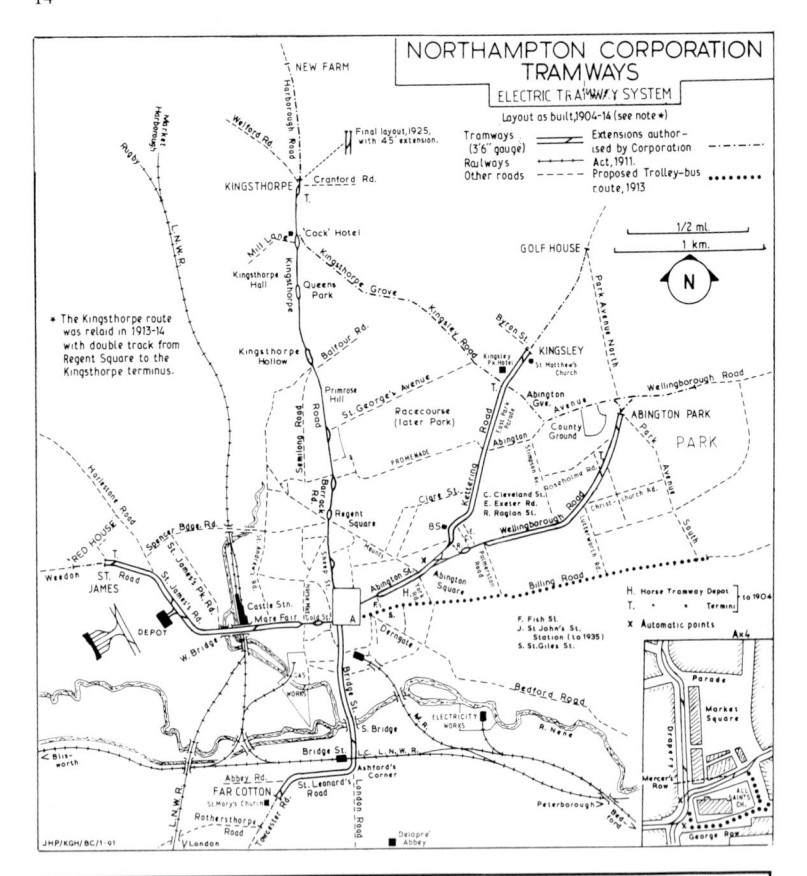

NORTHAMPTON CORPORATION TRANSPORT

NOTICE TO TRAMCAR DRIVERS   SINGLE DECK CARS

THE ATTENTION OF SINGLE DECK CAR DRIVERS IS ONCE AGAIN CALLED TO THE EXTRAORDINARY LENGTH OF THESE VEHICLES COMPARED TO THE SINGLE TRUCK CAR. THERE HAVE BEEN TWO OR THREE CASES JUST LATELY WHERE THE DRIVER RUNNING INTO THE ST. JAMES END TERMINUS HAS NOT ALLOWED THE REAR BOGIE SUFFICIENT CLEARANCE ON THE POINTS, ONLY TO FIND WHEN STARTING ON THE RETURN JOURNEY HE HAS ONE BOGIE ON EACH TRACK.

THIS SHOULD **NEVER** OCCUR IF DUE ATTENTION IS TAKEN BY THE DRIVER. IF YOU ARE IN ANY DOUBT EXAMINE THE POSITION OF THE TRAILING BOGIE BEFORE COMMENCING YOUR RETURN JOURNEY.

                       JOHN F. CAMERON, GENERAL MANAGER.

Tramways Offices,
February 21st 1931.

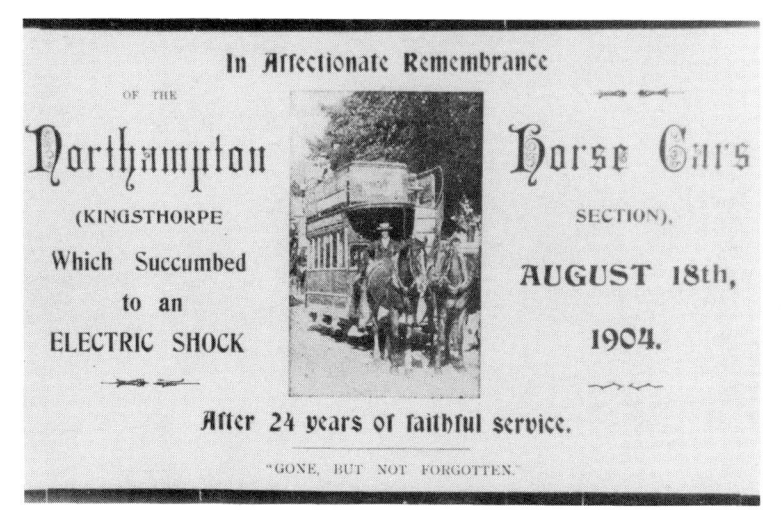

A souvenir postcard from the 1904 closure of Northampton's horse trams. *(C. Carter*

Northampton Corporation's inaugural electric cars at Abington Park on 21 July 1904.
(TMS

NORTHAMPTON

Mercer's Row, Northampton in 1928, with car No. 19 on the All Saints-Abington Park service and an open-top car for Kingsley.
(Science Museum Whitcombe Collection

Northampton single-decker 35 (series 34-37) in Mercers Row in 1928, en route from Kingsley to St. James.
(Science Museum Whitcombe Collection

Northampton 22 as rebuilt with extended platforms and canopies at The Drapery in 1928 on the Far Cotton-Kingsthorpe service.
(Science Museum Whitcombe Collection

Northampton 4 in Kettering Road at Cleveland Road corner on the Kingsley route.
(Commercial postcard, J. H. Price collection)

Northampton open-top car No. 3 on the steep gradient in Bridge Street in 1920, and Brush-built balcony car No. 28 at The Drapery in 1933. *(TMS, M. J. O'Connor)*

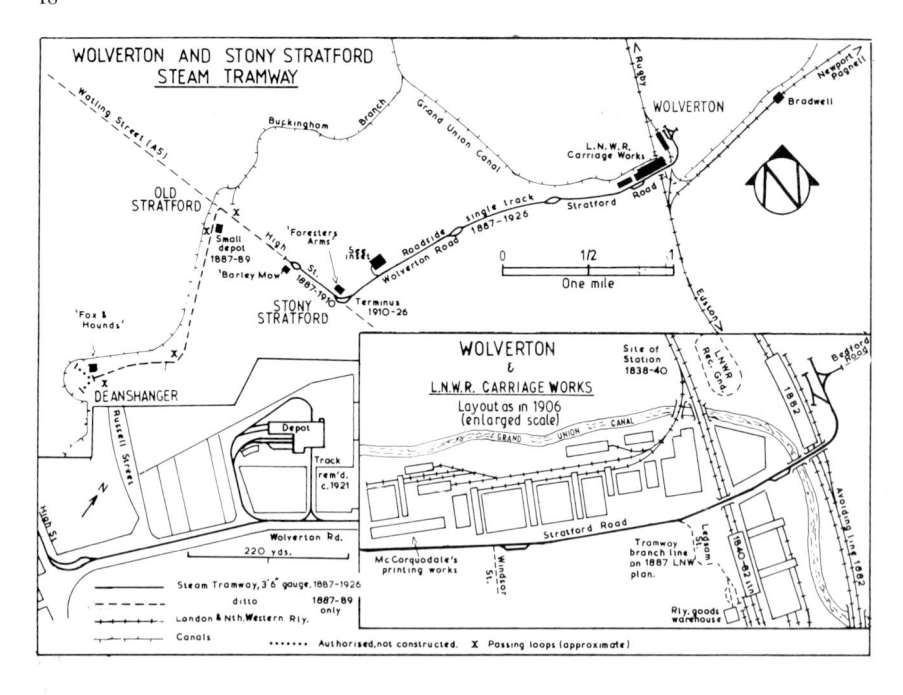

Krauss steam tram engine No. 3 of 1887 and trailer half-way between Wolverton and Stony Stratford. Most of the line ran on single track at the side of the main road.
(Commercial postcard, Lawson Series

19

One of the Wolverton & Stony Stratford Krauss engines with the 50-seat trailer at Deanshanger. This section of line opened in 1888 and closed a year later.
(Commercial postcard)

The Wolverton & Stony Stratford was unique among British steam tramways in being officially permitted to haul up to three trailers. Such trains were run for workmen at the London & North Western Railway's Wolverton carriage works.
(Commercial postcard, Hutchinson Series)

20

WOLVERTON AND STONY STRATFORD

Thomas Green engine and 100-seat trailer at Wolverton Station.
(TMS

Brush-built tram engine No. 4 and trailer at the Wolverton terminus.
(TMS

Bagnall engine No. 5 of 1922 at Stony Stratford after the tramway had been taken over by the London and North Western Railway.
(Commercial postcard

21

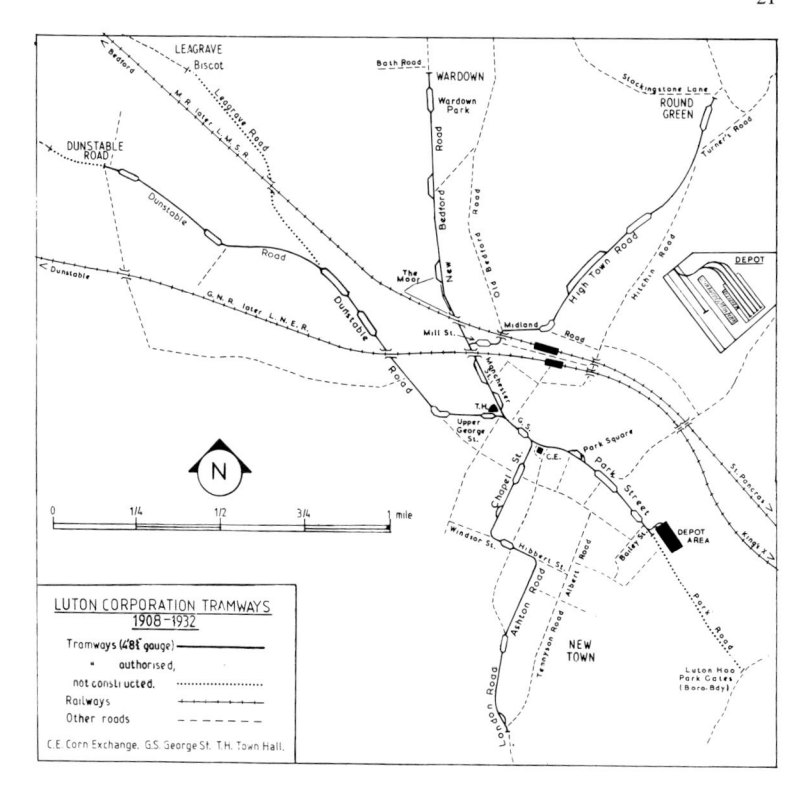

**LUTON CORPORATION TRAMWAYS
1908-1932**

Tramways (4'8½" gauge) ─────
  " authorised,
  not constructed. ....
Railways ┼┼┼┼┼┼
Other roads ─ ─ ─ ─ ─

C.E. Corn Exchange. G.S. George St. T.H. Town Hall.

"LUTON'S FIRST TRAM. Feb 21st - 08."

LUTON

Luton Corporation No. 3 at Bailey Street on 25 July 1931.
(G. N. Southerden)

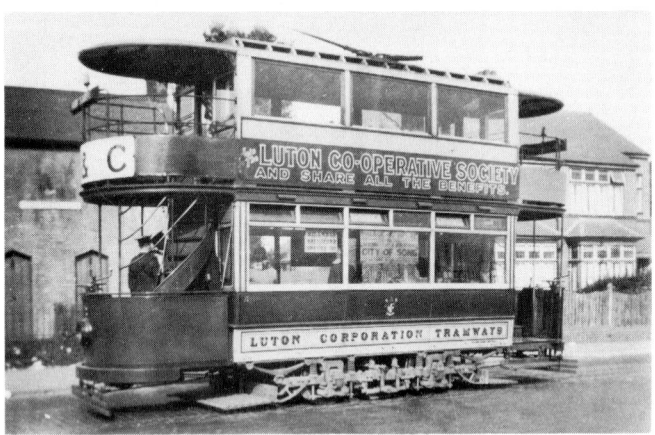

Luton 2 at Dunstable Road terminus. The four top-covered Luton cars (1, 2, 4, 5) were confined to this route, due to low bridges elsewhere.
(R. Elliott)

Luton 13, a former horse car motorised by Glasgow Corporation, at Luton's depot on 25 July 1931.
(G. N. Southerden)

23

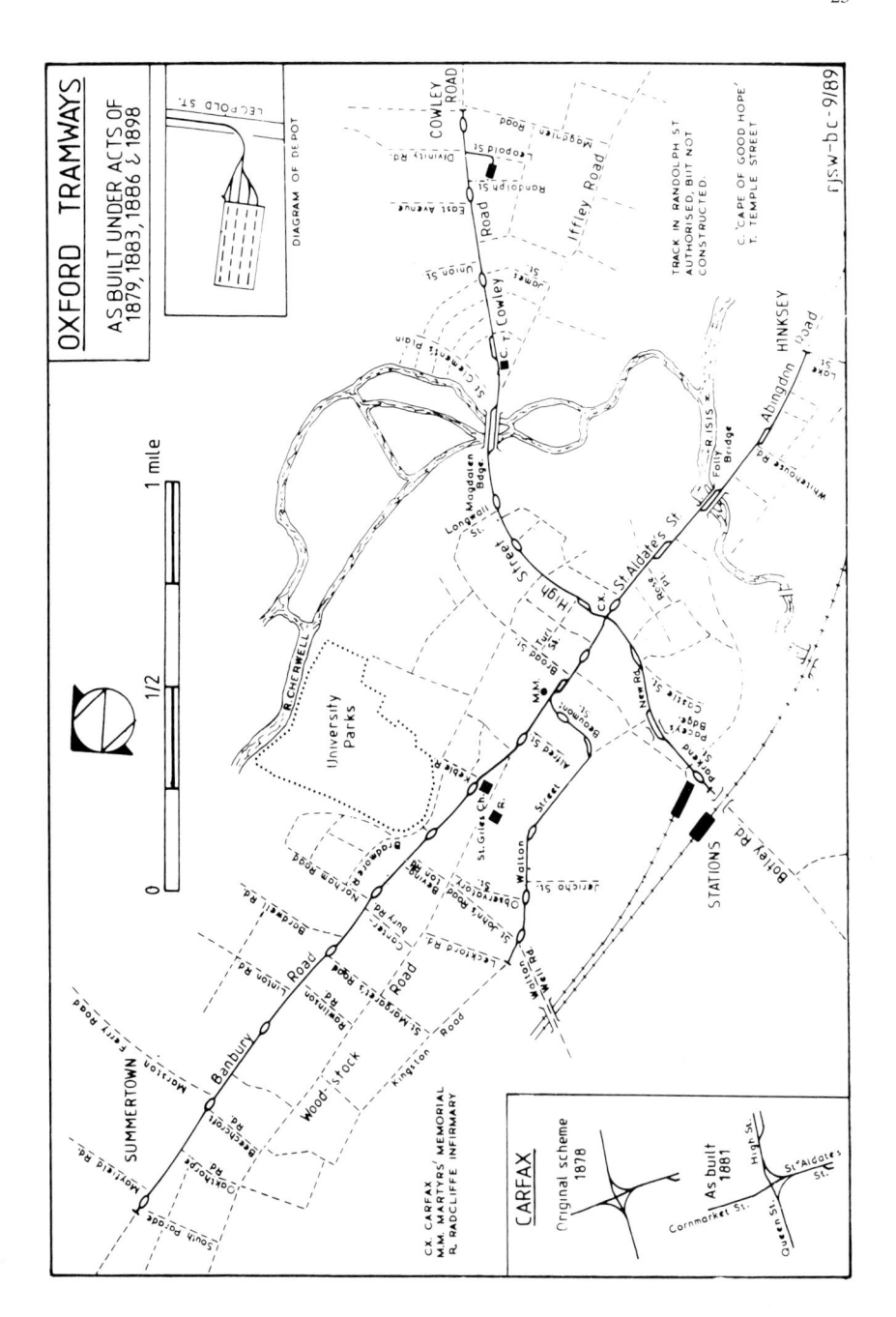

OXFORD

Two of Oxford's original 1881 horse cars in the High Street at Queen's Lane, about 1891.
(H. W. Taunt)

Knifeboard - seat double - decker No. 18 at Cowley Road terminus in September 1906.
(TMS)

An ex-London horse car at the Summertown terminus, with a ticket showing the post-1908 company title.
(TMS)

A knifeboard-seat Reading horse tram in the town centre (Broad Street) in the 1890s.
(Commercial postcard)

One of Reading Corporation's first thirty electric trams at Caversham Bridge soon after electric services began in the summer of 1903. This terminus was altered to a siding off the main road in 1927.
(Commercial postcard)

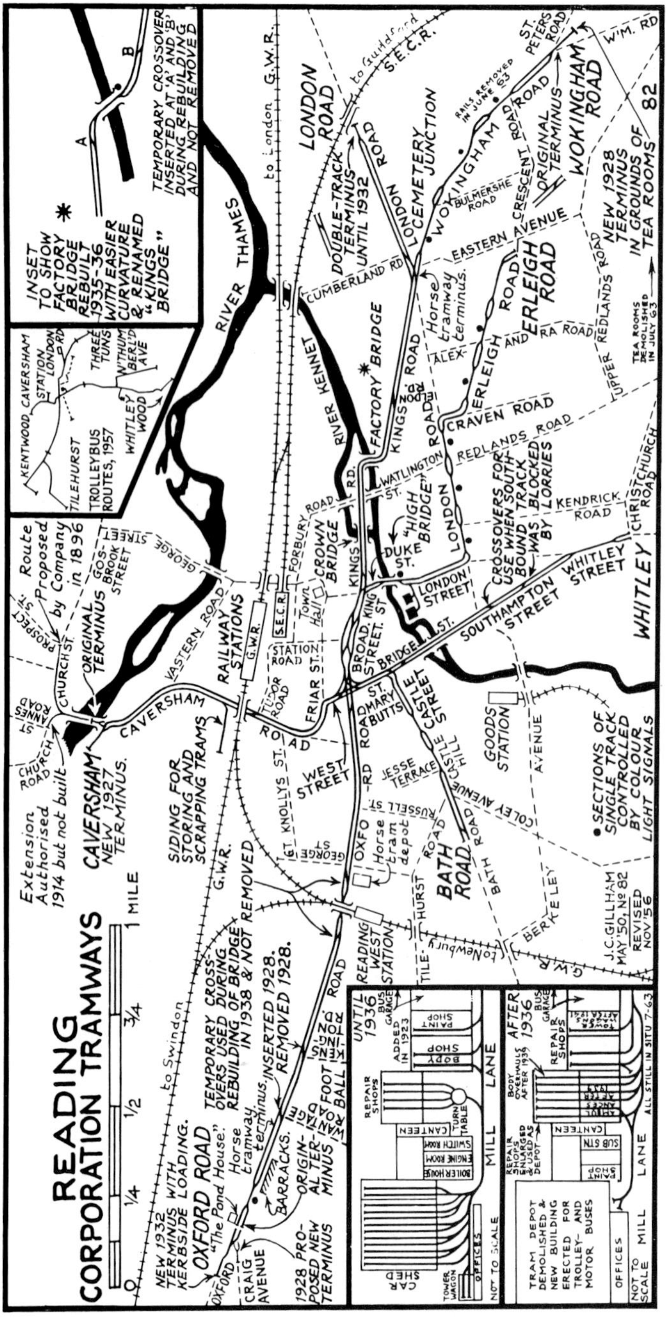

READING CORPORATION TRAMWAYS
0 1/4 1/2 3/4 1 MILE
Extension Authorised 1914 but not built
CAVERSHAM NEW 1927 TERMINUS.
Route Proposed by Company in 1896
ORIGINAL TERMINUS
INSET TO SHOW FACTORY BRIDGE REBUILT 1935-36 WITH EASIER CURVATURE & RENAMED "KINGS BRIDGE"
TEMPORARY CROSSOVER INSERTED AT 'A' AND 'B' DURING REBUILDING AND NOT REMOVED
TROLLEYBUS ROUTES, 1957
KENTWOOD
CAVERSHAM
STATION
LONDON RD
TILEHURST
THREE TUNS
N'THUM BERL'D AVE
WHITLEY WOOD
RIVER THAMES
RIVER KENNET
to London G.W.R.
to Guildford S.E.C.R.
LONDON ROAD
DOUBLE-TRACK TERMINUS UNTIL 1932
CEMETERY JUNCTION
RAILS REMOVED IN JUNE '63
WOKINGHAM ROAD
ST. PETERS ROAD
W'M. RD
ORIGINAL TERMINUS
CRESCENT ROAD
BULMERSHE ROAD
EASTERN AVENUE
ERLEIGH ROAD
NEW 1928 TERMINUS IN GROUNDS OF TEA ROOMS
TEA ROOMS DEMOLISHED IN JULY '63
82
CUMBERLAND RD
Horse tramway terminus.
FACTORY BRIDGE
KINGS ROAD
ELDON RD.
ALEX- AND RA ROAD
UPPER REDLANDS ROAD
CRAVEN ROAD
REDLANDS ROAD
WATLINGTON ST.
"HIGH BRIDGE"
DUKE ST.
LONDON ROAD
KENDRICK ROAD
CHRISTCHURCH ROAD
CROSSOVERS FOR USE WHEN SOUTH BOUND TRACK WAS BLOCKED BY LORRIES
LONDON STREET
WHITLEY STREET
WHITLEY
SOUTHAMPTON STREET
BRIDGE ST.
BROAD ST.
KING ST.
CROWN BRIDGE
FORBURY ROAD
Town Hall
S.E.C.R.
G.W.R.
RAILWAY STATIONS
STATION ROAD
FRIAR ST.
TUDOR ROAD
VASTERN ROAD
GEORGE STREET
GOS-BROOK STREET
PROSPECT ST.
CHURCH ST.
ST. ANNES ROAD
CHURCH ROAD
CAVERSHAM ROAD
SIDING FOR STORING AND SCRAPPING TRAMS
WEST STREET
ST. MARY BUTTS
CASTLE STREET
CASTLE HILL
JESSE TERRACE
KNOLLYS ST.
GT. GEORGE ST
RUSSELL ST.
COLEY AVENUE
GOODS STATION
AVENUE
SECTIONS OF SINGLE TRACK CONTROLLED BY COLOUR LIGHT SIGNALS
OXFORD ROAD
Horse tram depot
TILEHURST ROAD
BATH ROAD
BERKELEY
to Newbury G.W.R.
J.C. GILLHAM MAY '50, No 82 REVISED NOV '56
READING WEST STATION
G.W.R.
to Swindon
TEMPORARY CROSS-OVERS USED DURING REBUILDING OF BRIDGE IN 1938 & NOT REMOVED
INSERTED 1928. REMOVED 1928.
NEW 1932 TERMINUS WITH KERBSIDE LOADING.
OXFORD ROAD "The Pond House".
Horse tramway terminus.
BARRACKS.
ORIGIN-AL TER-MINUS
WANTAGE ROAD
FOOTBALL
KENS-INGTON RD.
1928 PRO-POSED NEW TERMINUS
CRAIG AVENUE
OXFORD
UNTIL 1936
BUS GARAGE
ADDED IN 1923
PAINT SHOP
BODY SHOP
REPAIR SHOPS
TURN TABLE
CANTEEN
SWITCH ROOM
ENGINE ROOM
BOILER HOUSE
CAR SHED
TOWER WAGON
OFFICES
MILL LANE
NOT TO SCALE
AFTER 1936
REPAIR SHOPS
BODY OVERHAULS AFTER 1936
REPAIR SHOPS ENLARGED & USED AS DEPOT
SUB STN
PAINT SHOP
TRAM DEPOT DEMOLISHED & NEW BUILDING ERECTED FOR TROLLEY- AND MOTOR BUSES
OFFICES
MILL LANE
ALL STILL IN SITU 7-63

READING

No. 7 at Wokingham Road terminus in 1939, showing new poles erected for trolleybus wires. All except one of Reading's 30 four-wheel trams had been rebuilt to this four-window design in the 1920s.
(W. A. Camwell)

One of the six Reading bogie cars (31-36) at Mill Lane depot in the mid-1930s, probably on football duty.
(G. N. Southerden)

Reading tram No. 5 decorated for the 1937 Coronation. (Reading Libraries)

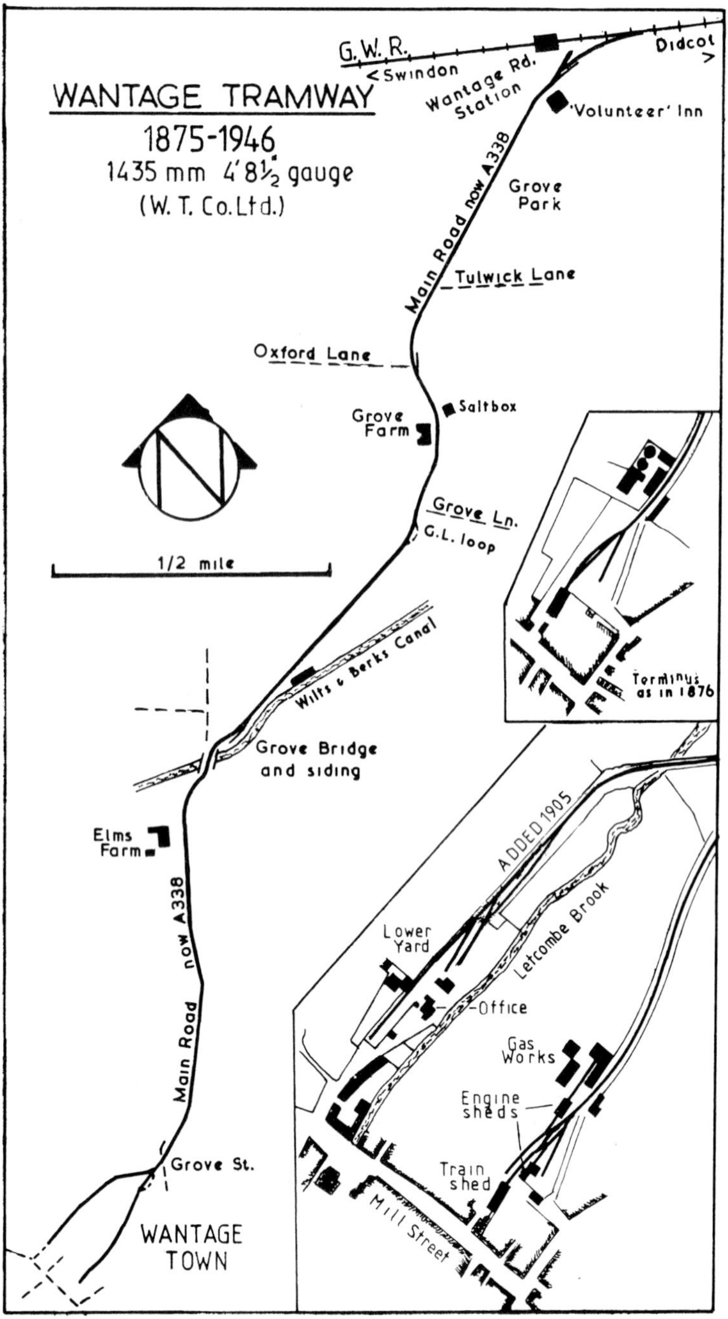
WANTAGE TRAMWAY
1875-1946
1435 mm 4'8½" gauge
(W. T. Co. Ltd.)
G.W.R.
<Swindon
Didcot >
Wantage Rd. Station
'Volunteer' Inn
Main Road now A338
Grove Park
Tulwick Lane
Oxford Lane
Saltbox
Grove Farm
Grove Ln.
G.L. loop
1/2 mile
Wilts & Berks Canal
Grove Bridge and siding
Terminus as in 1876
ADDED 1905
Elms Farm
Lower Yard
Letcombe Brook
Office
Gas Works
Engine sheds
Train shed
Mill Street
Grove St.
WANTAGE TOWN

WANTAGE

The Hughes tram engine of 1877 with trailers 1 and 3, about 1911.
(R. T. Reveley)

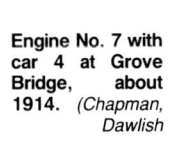

Engine No. 7 with car 4 at Grove Bridge, about 1914. (Chapman, Dawlish)

Engine No. 6 with cars 3 and 5 at Wantage in August 1924.
(F. Merton Atkins)

WANTAGE

John Grantham's self-propelled steam car in the form in which it arrived at Wantage in 1875. A model in the Science Museum shows it with a canvas roof.

Tram engine No. 6 with trailers 5 and 4 on the Orchard siding at Wantage in 1930, five years after passenger service had ceased.
(Science Museum, Whitcombe Collection

The last journey, May 1946, with goods engine No. 7 hauling No. 5 to Wantage Road station. No. 5 is now preserved, but No. 7 was scrapped in 1963 after industrial service. *(H. Evans*

WANTAGE

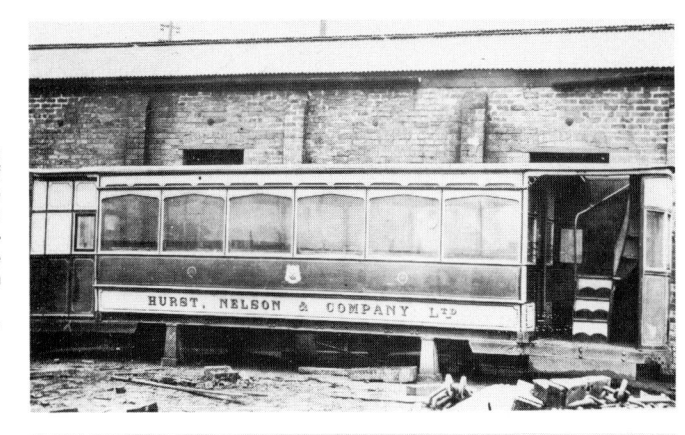

The Hurst Nelson exhibition car of 1900 at the builder's works in Motherwell. It became Wantage Tramway No. 4 in 1912.
(Hurst Nelson & Co.)

The Wantage Tramway Company also bought this Hurst Nelson saloon tram of 1902, seen here at Motherwell bearing the Bradford Corporation coat-of-arms.
(Hurst Nelson & Co.)

The same car as delivered to Wantage in 1912. Nos. 4 and 5 may have been the only British trams with steam heating.
(Hurst Nelson & Co.)

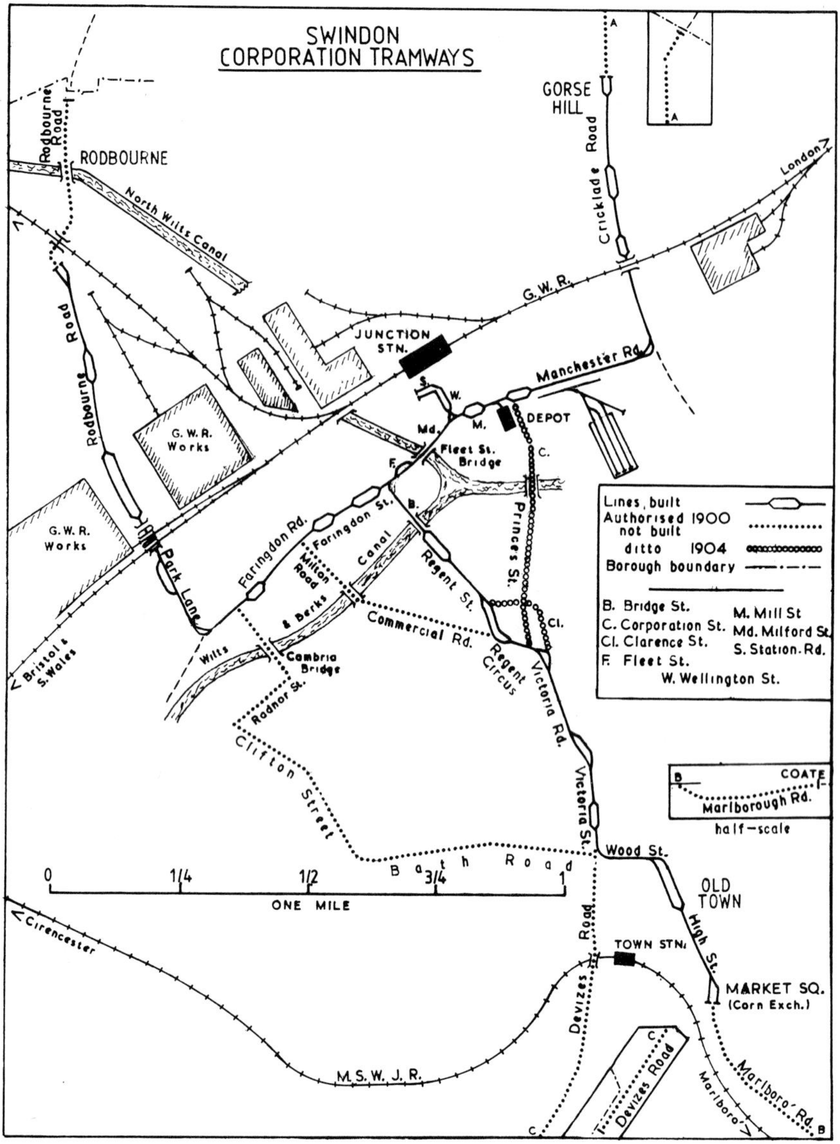
SWINDON
CORPORATION TRAMWAYS
GORSE HILL
Cricklade Road
Rodbourne Road
RODBOURNE
North Wilts Canal
London
G.W.R.
JUNCTION STN.
Manchester Rd.
DEPOT
G.W.R. Works
G.W.R. Works
Fleet St. Bridge
Faringdon Rd.
Faringdon St.
Milton Road
Canal
Regent St.
Princes St.
Park Lane
Wilts & Berks
Commercial Rd.
Regent Circus
Cambria Bridge
Radnor St.
Victoria Rd.
Clifton Street
Victoria St.
Wood St.
Bath Road
Bristol & S. Wales
OLD TOWN
High St.
MARKET SQ. (Corn Exch.)
TOWN STN.
Devizes Road
Cirencester
M.S.W.J.R.
Marlboro' Rd.
Marlboro'
0 1/4 1/2 3/4 1
ONE MILE
Lines, built
Authorised 1900 not built
ditto 1904
Borough boundary
B. Bridge St.
C. Corporation St.
Cl. Clarence St.
F. Fleet St.
M. Mill St
Md. Milford St.
S. Station Rd.
W. Wellington St.
COATE
Marlborough Rd.
half-scale

33

SWINDON

Swindon tram No. 2 in Faringdon Road on 26 July 1923, on the Rodbourne route.
(F. Merton Atkins)

Swindon 8 at Gorse Hill terminus, showing an automatic trolley reverser.
(G. N. Southerden)

Swindon 4 at the depot, a few days after the tramways closed on 11 July 1929.
(Science Museum, Whitcombe Collection)

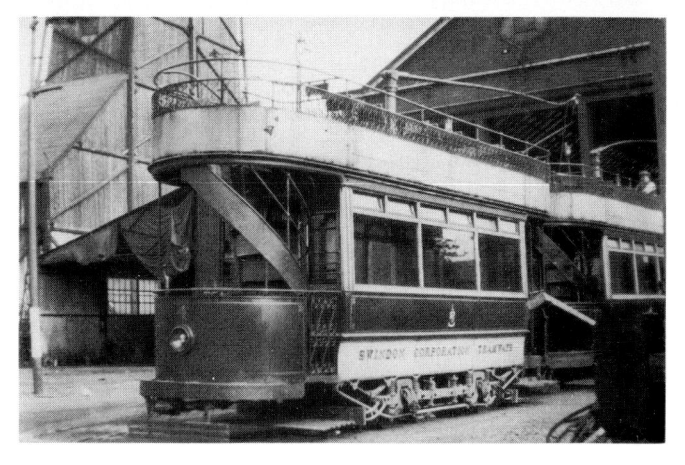

Swindon trams 1 and 13 in Regent Street in the 1920s. The body of No. 13 still exists near Gloucester.
(Commercial postcard)

Charleroi trailer 38, one of three cars imported from Belgium in 1973 for service at Cotswold Marina, South Cerney (Nos. 38, 41, 42). They are now on the Shane's Castle Railway in Northern Ireland.
(A. M. Keef)

A Gloucester one-horse tram, with the horse changing ends at the terminus in Southgate Street, about 1900. In the background are two open-sided cross-bench cars.
(Pamlin Prints)

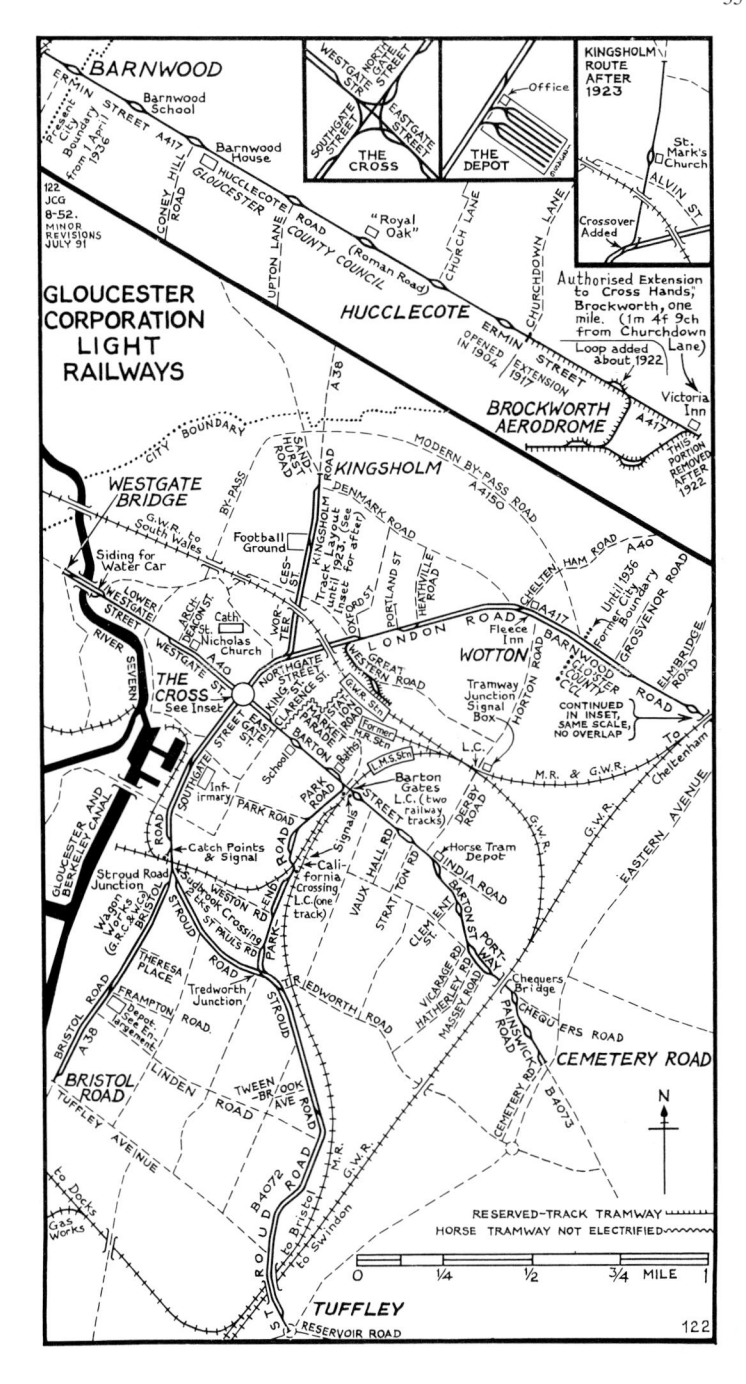

GLOUCESTER CORPORATION LIGHT RAILWAYS

GLOUCESTER

Gloucester Corporation trams 2 and 4 on test at Tuffley early in 1904. *(S. Pitcher)*

A Gloucester tram decorated for the 1911 Coronation.
(Courtesy, A. D. Packer)

Gloucester 14 and 12 at Hucclecote terminus in June 1929. From about 1915 to closure in 1933 the trams were painted all-over plain grey.
(Science Museum, Whitcombe Collection)

37

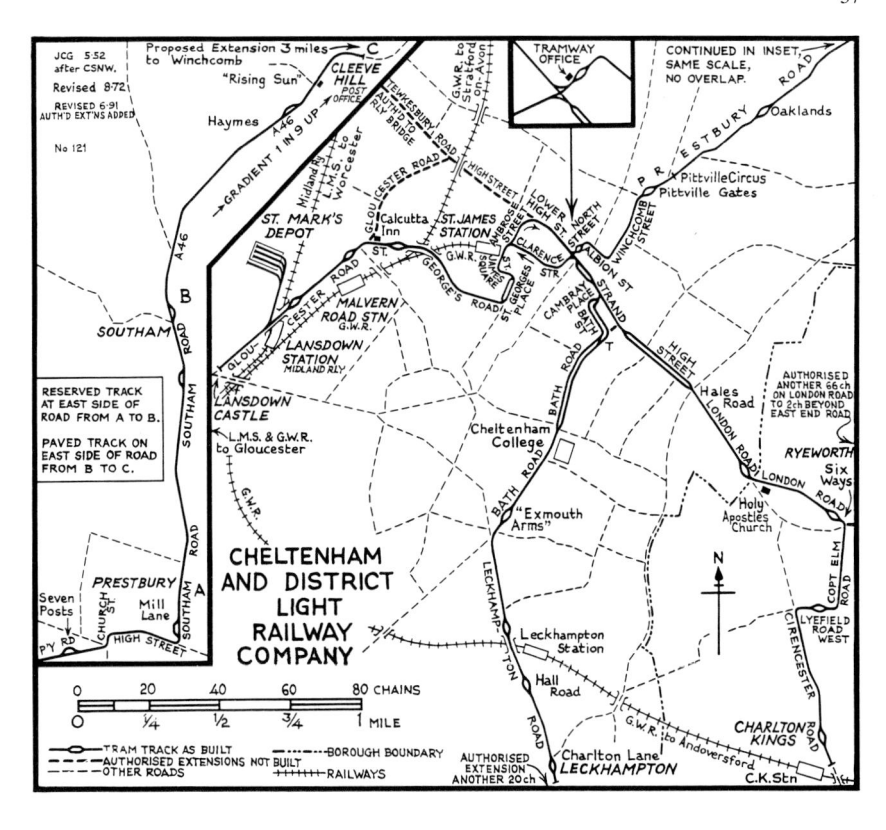

Restored Chelt-
enham tram 21 at
Crich in October
1963. After some
years later storage
in Bournemouth it
has now returned
to Cheltenham.
(R. B. Parr)

CHELTENHAM

One of Cheltenham & District's first eight trams, built in the USA in 1901. *(TMS)*

The next four Cheltenham trams (9-12) were built by the Gloucester Railway Carriage & Wagon Co. Ltd. in 1902.
(Gloucester RC&W)

Two Cheltenham trams (originally 9 and 10, later 3 and 12) ran as single-deckers on the steep Cleeve Hill route. *(TMS)*

CHELTENHAM

Car No. 13 was one of eight built by the British Electric Car Co. Ltd. of Trafford Park, Manchester in 1904 and is seen here at Charlton Kings terminus in 1929.
(Science Museum, Whitcombe Collection)

Cheltenham 21 to 23 were built by English Electric in 1921. This scene is at St. Mark's depot.
(B. R. Miller)

Three cars of Cheltenham's 13-20 series were rebuilt as shown here. No. 16 seen here approaching St. James Station was rebuilt in 1928.
(Science Museum, Whitcombe Collection)

A wagon of the Stratford and Moreton Tramway preserved and dislayed in Stratford - on - Avon. *(J. H. Price)*

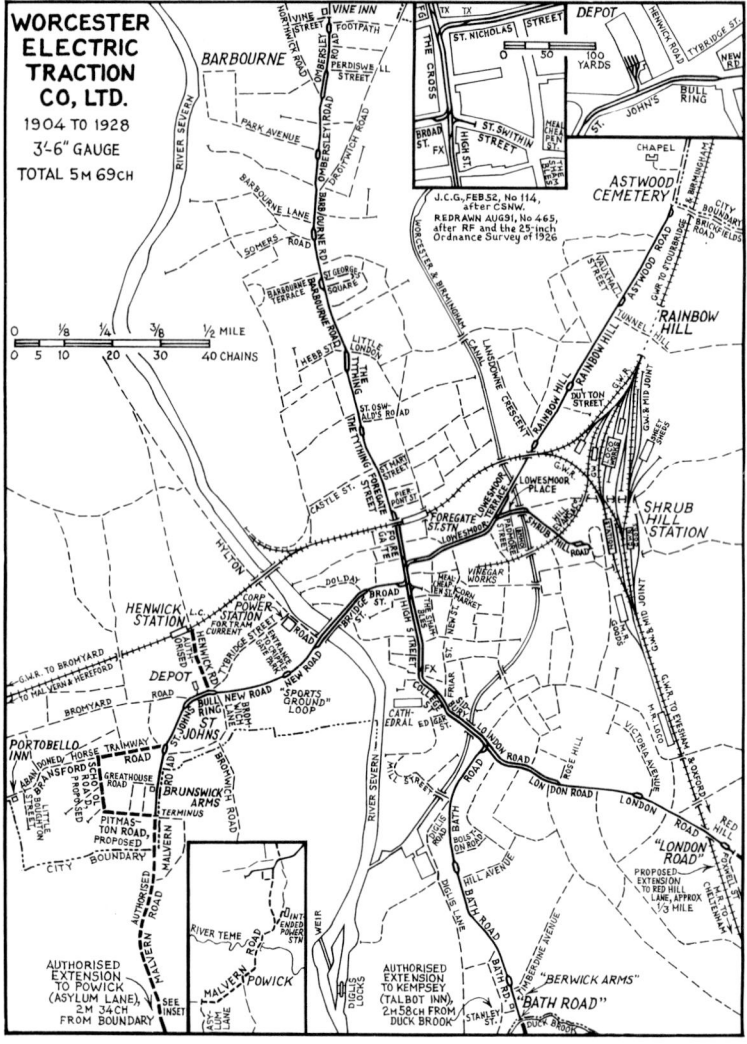

A turn-of-century view of The Cross, Worcester, with two double-deck horse cars, a cross-bench single-decker and a horse bus.
(Commercial postcard, J. H. Price collection)

The Worcester Electric Traction Co. Ltd., had a fleet of 17 trams. Fifteen of them were built by Brush in 1904, of the type shown in the left-hand photograph of No. 6. The final pair, 16 and 17, were built for Worcester by the Birmingham and Midland Tramways at their Tividale Works in 1921. *(TMS and H. V. Jinks)*

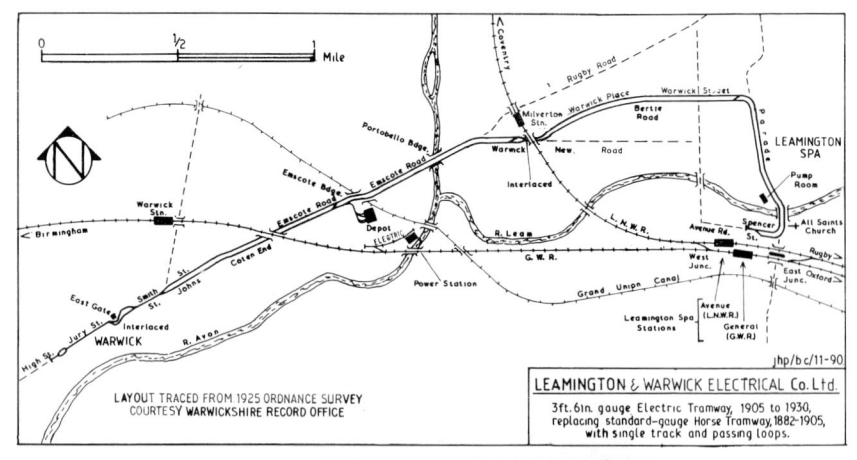

LAYOUT TRACED FROM 1925 ORDNANCE SURVEY
COURTESY WARWICKSHIRE RECORD OFFICE

LEAMINGTON & WARWICK ELECTRICAL Co. Ltd.
3ft. 6in. gauge Electric Tramway, 1905 to 1930, replacing standard-gauge Horse Tramway, 1882-1905, with single track and passing loops.

One of the nine Leamington and Warwick horse cars standing at the Leamington terminus.
(Courtesy, F. K. Farrell

Leamington and Warwick electric car No. 2 at Warwick terminus at the start of operation in July 1905. This tramway company did not provide uniforms.
(Lens of Sutton

LEAMINGTON AND WARWICK

No. 5, one of the original six cars of 1905, standing outside All Saints Church, Leamington Spa, in 1929.
(Science Museum, Whitcombe Collection)

Ex-Taunton car No. 8 at Leamington Spa (Avenue Road terminus) in 1929.
(Science Museum, Whitcombe Collection)

Car No. 14 of 1921 at the Warwick terminus shortly before tram operation ceased in 1930.
(G. N. Southerden)

Tramcar Fleet Lists

All cars were four-wheel double-deck unless otherwise stated.
Seating figures shown thus 22/26 are for lower and upper decks respectively.
The opening dates shown are the first day of regular public service.

Cheltenham & District Light Railway Company

10.44 miles, 3ft 6in gauge, opened 17 August 1901, closed 31 December 1930. Livery: red and primrose (cars 1-12 originally all-over dark red).

Car Numbers	Type (as built)	Year Built	Builder	Seats	Truck(s)	Motors	Controllers
1-8	Open top	1901	Stephenson	22/26	Peckham Cantilever (b)	Westinghouse 2 x 30 hp	Westinghouse
9-12 (note a)	Open top	1902	Gloucester	22/26 (note a)	Peckham Cantilever (b)	Westinghouse 2 x 30 hp	Westinghouse
13-20	Open top	1904	BEC	22/26	Peckham Cantilever (b)	GE 58-6T 2 x 28 hp	BTH B18
21-23 (note c)	Open top	1921	EE	20/32	Preston Peckham Pendulum	MV 323 2 x 35 hp	Westinghouse T1/C
24, 25 (note d)	Open top	(bought 1928)	BMTJC	22/28	Brill 21E (Brush?)	DK 25B 2 x 28 hp	EE DB1 K3

Notes
(a) Two cars (initially 9 and 10) ran as 28-seat single-deck cars (with stairs and top seats removed, and extra seats on platforms). From c. 1920 the two single-deck cars were Nos. 3 and 12.
(b) Cars 1-4, 7-9, 14-16 and 19 later received Brill 21E trucks. 14 renumbered 10 in 1927, 19 renumbered 1 in 1928.
(c) This order was for four cars but one was diverted to Leamington & Warwick (No. 14).
(d) Bought in 1928 from Worcester Electric Traction Co. Ltd. (Nos. 16 and 17).

Gloucester Tramways Company Ltd.

3.40 miles, 4ft 0in gauge, opened 24 May 1879, sold to City of Gloucester Tramways Co. Ltd. July 1881, municipalised 1 January 1903, closed 17 March 1904. Maximum horse-car fleet, 14 single-deck cars, by Bristol, Brush, Gloucester and Starbuck.

Gloucester Corporation Light Railways

9.75 miles (maximum), 3ft 6in gauge, opened 29 April 1904 (ceremonial opening 3 May 1904), closed 11 January 1933. Livery: crimson lake and cream; all-over light grey from 1915 to 1933. Mileage includes 2.69 miles owned by Gloucestershire County Council, but 0.62 of this was with rails removed from abandoned Westgate route.

Car Numbers	Type (as built)	Year Built	Builder	Seats	Truck(s)	Motors	Controllers
1-20	Open top	1903/4	Brush	18/23	Brush AA	DK 25B 2 x 25 hp	DK DB1 Form C
21-30	Open top	1904	Brush	18/23	Brush AA	Brush	Brush
Water car/ grinder	2000 gallons	1905	ER&TCW	—	Brush A	DK 25B 2 x 25 hp	DK DB1 Form C ?

Leamington & Warwick Tramways & Omnibus Company, Ltd.

3.00 miles, 4ft 8½in gauge, horse traction, opened 21 November 1881, closed 15 March 1905. Maximum nine cars, built by Metropolitan, Brown Marshall, and Midland.

Leamington & Warwick Electrical Company, Ltd.

3.05 miles, 3ft 6in gauge, opened 15 July 1905, closed 16 August 1930. Livery: holly green and cream.

Car Numbers	Type (as built)	Year Built	Builder	Seats	Truck(s)	Motors	Controllers
1-6	Open top	1905	Brush	22/26	Brush AA (note a, c)	Brush	Brush
7-12 (note b)	Open top	(Bought 1905)	Brush	22/29	Brush A (note c)	Brush 800 2 x 17 hp	Brush
14 (note d)	Open top	1921	EE	20/32	Preston Pendulum	MV 323 2 x 35 hp	Westinghouse T1/C

Notes
(a) BET Gazette lists these trucks as Brush Radial (contrary to photographs).
(b) Built 1901/2 for Taunton (series 1-6).
(c) Certain cars received Peckham Pendulum P22 trucks in the 1920s.
(d) Built as Cheltenham 24, diverted to Leamington as new.

Luton Corporation Tramways

5.25 miles, 4ft 8½in gauge, opened 21 February 1908 under lease, municipally operated from 21 February 1923, closed 16 April 1932. Livery: grass-green and ivory.

Car Numbers	Type (as built)	Year Built	Builder	Seats	Truck(s)	Motors	Controllers
1-12	Open top (note a)	1907/8	UEC	22/32	M&G 21EM	BTH GE54 2 x 29 hp	BTH K10D
13 (note b)	Single deck	(Bought 1923)	GCT	20 ?	Brill 21E	BTH GE52 2 x 20 hp	Westinghouse

Notes
(a) Cars 1, 2, 4, 5 were given Brush top covers in 1929.
(b) Bought from Glasgow May 1923 after serving as horse car, electric passenger car 118, and parcels car.

Northampton Street Tramways Company.

5.25 miles, 3ft 6in gauge, horse traction, opened 4 June 1881, municipalised 21 October 1901, closed 18 August 1904. Maximum 22 cars, mostly by BRCW.

Northampton Corporation Tramways

6.42 miles, 3ft 6in gauge, opened 21 July 1904, closed 15 December 1934. Livery: vermillion and white.

Car Numbers	Type (as built)	Year Built	Builder	Seats	Truck(s)	Motors	Controllers
1-20	Open top	1904	ER&TCW	22/24	Brill 21E	DK 25B 2 x 27 hp	DK DB1 Form C
21, 22	Open top	1905	ER&TCW	22/24	Brill 21E	DK 25B 2 x 27 hp	DK DB1 Form C
23, 24	Open top	1910	UEC	22/28	Brill 21E	DK 13B 2 x 30 hp	DK DB1 K3
25, 26	Open top	1911	UEC	22/28	Brill 21E	DK 13B 2 x 30 hp	DK DB1 K3
27-33	Balcony top	1914	Brush	22/26	Brush 21E	DK 13B 2 x 30 hp	DK DB1 K3
34-37	Single-deck bogie	1921	EE	42	Preston 22E bogies	DK 30B1 2 x 40 hp	EE DB1 K3B

Balcony top covers (by Brush) were fitted to cars 19 (1923), 5, 10, 13 (1925), 20, 21, 22 (1926).

City of Oxford and District Tramways Company, Ltd.

5.25 miles, 4ft 0in gauge, horse traction, opened 1 December 1881, transferred 1907 to City of Oxford Electric Tramways Ltd., closed 7 August 1914. Maximum 20 cars, originally eight single-deck, later all double-deck. Certain cars bought from London area tramways. Livery: dark red and white, some cars later brown and white.

Reading Tramways Company

2.37 miles, 4ft gauge, horse traction, opened 5 April 1879, municipalised 31 October 1901, closed 21 July 1903. Maximum thirteen cars, originally seven single-deck, later all double-deck.

Reading Corporation Tramways

7.45 miles, 4ft gauge, opened 22 July 1903, closed 20 May 1939. Livery: Crimson lake and cream.

Car Numbers	Type (as built)	Year Built	Builder	Seats	Truck(s)	Motors	Controllers
1-30	Open top	1903	ER&TCW	22/28	Brill 21E	DK 25A 2 x 25 hp	DK DB1 Form B
31-36	Open top bogie	1904	ER&TCW	30/40	Brill 22E bogies	DK 6A 2 x 35 hp	DK DB1 Form C
37	Water car/ rail grinder	1904	ER&TCW	—	Brill 21E	DK 25A 2 x 25 hp	DK DB1 Form C

Cars 31-36 were re-equipped in 1916 with DK20A 40 hp motors and K3 controllers.
Cars 1-9 and 11-30 were rebodied by RCT between 1920 and 1929; 14 of these cars received EE K3B controllers.
Cars 31 and 32 received MV102DR 50 hp motors in 1927. Car 30 received MV controllers.

The Reading trams were replaced by trolleybuses, which operated from 18 July 1936 to 2 November 1968 (closing ceremony on 3 November).

Swindon Corporation Tramways

3.70 miles, 3ft 6in gauge, opened 22 September 1904, closed 11 July 1929. Livery: maroon and cream.

Car Numbers	Type (as built)	Year Built	Builder	Seats	Truck(s)	Motors	Controllers
1-7	Open top	1904	ER&TCW	22/26	Brill 21E	DK 6A 2 x 35 hp	DK DB1 Form E
8, 9	Open top	1905	ER&TCW	22/26	Brill 21E	DK 6A 2 x 35 hp	DK DB1 Form E
10-12	Open top	1906	Brush	54	Brush Conaty	Brush 2 x 32 hp	Brush
13	Open top	1921	EE	54	Preston Standard	DK 29A 2 x 30 hp	EE DB1 K4

Wantage Tramway Company Limited

2.47 miles, 4ft 8½in gauge, opened with horse traction (cars 1, 2) 11 October 1875, largely steam from 1 August 1876 (wholly steam from mid-1880s), closed to passengers 31 July 1925, to goods 21 December 1945. Cars brown, engines green.

Vehicle	Type	Year Built	Year Bought	Builder	Works Number	Seats	Withdrawn	Scrapped
Grantham car	Combined steam car	1872	1876	Oldbury and Merryweather	—	c. 48 ?	1890	1891
Engine No. 4	Tram engine	1877	1877	Hughes	7		1919	1920
Engine No. 5	Goods engine	1857	1878	George England	—	—	1945	(Preserved)
Engine No. 6	Matthews tram engine	1880	1888	(Kingsbury ?)	—	—	1925	1931
Engine No. 7	Goods engine	1888	1893	Manning Wardle	1057	—	1945	1963
Engine 1329	Goods engine	1874	1910	Avonside	1052	—	1919	1920
The Driver	Goods engine	1875	1919	Manning Wardle	515	—	1920	1920
Car No. 1	Small single deck (ex d/d)	1875	1875	Starbuck	—	16?	1919	?
Car No. 2	Small s/deck	1875	1876	Starbuck	—	16?	1919	?
Car No. 3	Longer s/deck	1890	1890	Milnes	—	20?	1925	1930
Car No. 4 (i) Car No. 5 (i)	Ex-Reading horse cars	c.1891	1903	?	—	16?	1912	?
Car No. 4 (ii)	Bogie single deck (a)	1900	1912	Hurst Nelson	—	30	1925	1931
Car No. 5 (ii)	Single deck saloon (b)	1902	1912	Hurst Nelson	—	22	1925	1931

All the engines were of 0-4-0 wheel arrangement. The Matthews engine had been tried on the Wantage Tramway in 1882-83.

A Merryweather tram engine (works No. 9/1876) was tried in 1876-77, and two Mekarski compressed-air cars in 1880.

Notes
(a) Built as double-deck electric exhibition car for British Thomson-Houston.
(b) Built as saloon tram for Bradford Corporation but order cancelled.

Worcester Tramways Company, Ltd.

3.27 miles, 3ft gauge, horse traction, opened 18 February 1884, transferred to Worcester Tramways Limited in 1894, closed 25 June 1903. Cars: six Falcon double-deck, two later single-deck cars, various secondhand double-deck c. 1900.

Worcester Electric Traction Company, Ltd.

5.86 miles, 3ft 6in gauge, opened 6 February 1904, closed 31 May 1928. Livery: Holly green and cream.

Car Numbers	Type (as built)	Year Built	Builder	Seats	Truck(s)	Motors	Controllers
1-15 (note a)	Open top	1904	Brush	22/28	Brush AA	DK 25B 2 x 28 hp	DK DB1 Form C
16, 17	Open top	1921	BMTJC	22/28	Brill 21E (Brush ?)	DK 25B 2 x 28 hp	EE DB1 K3

Notes
(a) Delivered in three 1904 batches (eight, five and two). Two other cars built for Worcester were diverted to Peterborough.
(b) Nos. 16 and 17 were sold to Cheltenham in 1928.

Wolverton and Stony Stratford Steam Tramway

2.67 miles (excluding 2.04 mile Deanshanger extension), 3ft 6in gauge, opened 27 May 1887, closed 19 May 1926 (on strike since 4 May). Livery: tawny brown (chocolate and white from 1920).

Vehicle	Type	Year Built	Builder	Works Number	Seats	Withdrawn
Engines 1 and 2	Tram engines	1887	Krauss	1861, 1862	—	1887
Engine No. 3	Tram engine	1887	Krauss	1863	—	c. 1920 ?
Engines 1, 2 (ii)	Tram engines	1887	Thomas Green	43, 51	—	1926
Engine No. 4	Tram engine	1904	Brush	308	—	1926
Engine No. 5	Saddle tank	1922	Bagnall	2153	—	1926
Three cars	Bogie double deck	1887	Midland	—	100	1926
One car	Bogie double deck	1887	Midland	—	80	1926
One car	Bogie double deck	1888	Midland	—	50	1926
One car	Single deck cross bench	1888	Midland	—	20?	1889

A fourth Krauss tram engine (works number 1864) was ordered but not taken into stock.
The original stock also incldued 10 wagons and some parcels vans.
The trailer cars were not externally numbered, except for 100-seat car 2 post-1921.

Key to Abbreviations and Manufacturers

Bagnall	—	W. G. Bagnall & Co Ltd, Stafford.
Brill	—	The J. G. Brill Company, Philadelphia, USA.
BEC	—	The British Electric Car Co Ltd, Trafford Park, Manchester.
BET	—	The British Electric Traction Co Limited.
BMTJC	—	Birmingham & Midland Tramways Joint Committee, Tividale Works.
BRCW	—	The Birmingham Railway Carriage & Wagon Co Ltd, Smethwick.
Bristol	—	The Bristol Wagon & Carriage Works Ltd, Lawrence Hill, Bristol.
Brush	—	The Brush Electrical Engineering Co Ltd, Loughborough.
BTH	—	British Thomson-Houston Co Ltd, Rugby.
DK	—	Dick, Kerr & Co Ltd, Preston.
Dolter	—	Dolter Electric Traction Limited, London E.C.
EE	—	The English Electric Co Ltd, Preston.
ER&TCW	—	The Electric Railway & Tramway Carriage Works Ltd, Preston.
GCT	—	Glasgow Corporation Tramways, Coplawhill Works.
Falcon	—	The Falcon Engine & Car Works, Loughborough (to Brush Co, 1889).
GE	—	The General Electric Company, Schenectady, USA.
Gloucester	—	Gloucester Railway Carriage & Wagon Co Ltd, Gloucester.
GWR	—	Great Western Railway Company.
Hughes	—	(Manufactured by Falcon Engine & Car Works, Loughborough).
Hurst Nelson	—	Hurst Nelson & Co Ltd, Motherwell, Scotland.
Kingsbury	—	Kingsbury Ironworks, Ball's Pond, London.
Krauss	—	Lokomotivfabrik Krauss & Cie, München.
LMSR	—	London Midland and Scottish Railway Company.
LNWR	—	London and North Western Railway Company.
Manning Wardle	—	Manning Wardle & Co Ltd, Locomotive Builders, Leeds.
Metropolitan	—	The Metropolitan Railway Carriage & Wagon Co. Ltd., Saltley.
Midland	—	Midland Railway-Carriage & Wagon Co Ltd, Shrewsbury.
Milnes	—	Geo. F. Milnes & Co Ltd, Birkenhead.
M & G	—	Mountain & Gibson Ltd, Bury, Lancashire.
MV	—	Metropolitan-Vickers Electrical Co Ltd, Trafford Park, Manchester.
Oldbury	—	Oldbury Railway Carriage & Wagon Co. Ltd., Oldbury, Worcs.
Peckham	—	Trucks built by or for the Peckham Truck & Engineering Co Ltd.
RCT	—	Reading Corporation Tramways, Mill Lane depot and works.
Starbuck	—	George Starbuck & Company, Birkenhead.
Stephenson	—	The John Stephenson Company, New York, USA.
Thomas Green	—	Thomas Green & Sons Ltd, Leeds.
T&RW	—	*The Tramway and Railway World.*
TMS	—	The Tramway Museum Society.
UEC	—	United Electric Car Co Ltd, Preston.
Walker	—	The Walker Electric Company, Cleveland, USA.
Westinghouse	—	Westinghouse Electric Co Ltd, Trafford Park, Manchester.

The Electric Railway & Tramway Carriage Works Ltd (renamed United Electric Car Company Ltd from 25 September 1905) was a subsidiary of Dick, Kerr & Co Ltd, which merged with other electrical companies on 14 December 1918 to form the English Electric Co Ltd.

Acknowledgments and Bibliography

The text of this book is based on the regional chapters of *Great British Tramway Networks* by W. H. Bett and J. C. Gillham, which was published in four successive editions by the Light Railway Transport League. These are now out of print, but the chapters are being republished in the form of regional booklets, of which this is the eighth, and combines parts of former chapters 7, 8 and 11.

The text has been revised and enlarged as necessary in the light of new research, based partly on the new works listed in the bibliography, and partly on recent work by J. C. Gillham and J. H. Price. The fleet lists on pages 44 to 47 have been compiled by J. H. Price, with the valued assistance of F. P. Groves, M. J. Russell, N. Taylor and J. S. Webb. The locomotive lists for Wantage and Wolverton have been compiled by G. E. Baddeley, with assistance from G. S. Moore and N. Kelly. J. C. Gillham and A. A. Jackson each provided many entries for the Bibliography.

The maps of Cheltenham, Gloucester, Reading, Stroud, Wellingborough and Worcester were drawn by J. C. Gillham, and the other maps were drawn for this book by Brian Connelly, with assistance from J. C. Gillham, K. G. Harvie, A. A. Jackson, J. H. Price and H. E. Pryer. Good use has been made of material held by the Local Studies libraries at Leamington Spa, Luton, Northampton, Oxford and Worcester, to whom we record our thanks. Many of the relevant Acts of Parliament, Light Railway Orders, and 25-inch Ordnance Survey maps have also been studied.

A number of the illustrations are reproduced from *The Tramway Review* or from earlier books which are now out of print. Others have not been published before, and in both cases we are grateful to all the photographers or copyright owners for permission to reproduce their work, and to David Packer and Major C. S. N. Walker for their help in locating suitable prints. Photographs marked TMS are reproduced by permission of the Tramway Museum Society, from the R. B. Parr collection, and those taken by the late Dr. H. A. Whitcombe are reproduced by courtesy of the Science Museum.

Periodicals consulted have included *Modern Tramway, Tramway Review, Modern Transport, The Light Railway & Tramway Journal, The Tramway and Railway World, The Electrician, The Electrical Review* and *The B.E.T. Gazette*.

The next book in this series will deal with the tramways of Kent, including those in the North Kent outskirts of London.

Bibliography — General

Great British Tramway Networks, by W. H. Bett and J. C. Gillham (Light Railway Transport League, fourth edition, 1962). The present work is based on extracts from this book, greatly augmented.

Tramways of the West of England, by P. W. Gentry. First edition 1952, second edition published 1960 by Light Railway Transport League. Includes chapters on Cheltenham, Gloucester, Swindon and Worcester.

West Country Electric Trams, by J. B. Appleby (Transport Publishing Company, Glossop, 1975).

Tramways Remembered — South and South West England, by L. Oppitz (Countryside Books, Newbury, 1990).